ISAAC ASIMOV'S
Library of the Universe

Neptune:
The Farthest Giant

by Isaac Asimov

Gareth Stevens Publishing
Milwaukee

The reproduction rights to all photographs and illustrations in this book are controlled by the individuals or institutions credited on page 32 and may not be reproduced without their permission.

The publishers gratefully acknowledge the generous assistance of Jurie van der Woude and the staff of Jet Propulsion Laboratory.

Library of Congress Cataloging-in-Publication Data

Asimov, Isaac, 1920-
    Neptune : the farthest giant / Isaac Asimov.
       p.   cm. — (Isaac Asimov's Library of the universe)
    Includes bibliographical references.
    Summary: Describes the characteristics and movements of the planet Neptune and how we found out about it.
    ISBN 1-55532-369-3
    1. Neptune (Planet)—Juvenile literature. [1. Neptune (Planet)] I. Title. II. Series: Asimov, Isaac, 1920- Library of the universe.
    QB691.A85   1990
    523.4'81—dc20   89-43136

A Gareth Stevens Children's Books edition

Edited, designed, and produced by
Gareth Stevens, Inc.
RiverCenter Building, Suite 201
1555 North RiverCenter Drive
Milwaukee, Wisconsin 53212, USA

For a free color catalog describing Gareth Stevens' list of high-quality children's books, call 1-800-341-3569 (USA) or 1-800-461-9120 (Canada).

Cover art © Bob Eggleton 1990

Project editor: Mark Sachner
Series design: Laurie Shock
Book design: Kate Kriege
Research editors: Scott Enk and John D. Rateliff
Picture editor: Matthew Groshek
Editorial assistant: Diane Laska
Technical advisers and consulting editors: Julian Baum and Francis Reddy

Printed in the United States of America

1 2 3 4 5 6 7 8 9 96 95 94 93 92 91 90

CONTENTS

Nowadays, we have seen planets up close, all except for the farthest planet, Pluto. We have mapped Venus through its clouds. We have seen dead volcanoes on Mars and live ones on Io, one of Jupiter's satellites. We have detected strange objects no one knew anything about till recently: quasars, pulsars, black holes. We have studied stars not only by the light they give out, but by other kinds of radiation: infrared, ultraviolet, x-rays, radio waves. We have even detected tiny particles called neutrinos that are given off by the stars.

And in August 1989, a probe called Voyager 2 completed a 12-year journey to the outer planets by passing close to the distant planet Neptune and its largest satellite, Triton. It has sent us back interesting information about these far-off worlds. In this book we will tell you about Neptune.

Isaac Asimov

A Double Beginning

By the 1840s, it was clear that the motion of the most distant planet then known, Uranus, was not quite what it should be.

Two astronomers, John Couch Adams of England and Urbain Jean Joseph Leverrier of France, working separately, each felt there must be a planet beyond Uranus that pulled at it and affected its motion. Each one calculated where the other planet might be.

In 1846, two German astronomers, Johann Gottfried Galle and Heinrich Ludwig d'Arrest, looked where Leverrier had told them to look — and at once they found a planet close to the spot that Leverrier had predicted. The planet had a bluish green appearance, so it was named Neptune, for the Roman god of the sea. Today, like Galle and d'Arrest, both Adams and Leverrier are generally given a share of the credit for the discovery of Neptune.

French mathematician Urbain Leverrier (above) and British astronomer John Couch Adams (below) discovered Neptune mathematically.

Opposite: the blue face of Neptune, last of the giant planets. Bright cirrus clouds constantly attend the dark oval of an Earth-sized storm in Neptune's atmosphere.

Planet, planet — who is the fastest of them all?

Earth speeds about the Sun at 18.6 miles (29.9 km) per second. That's much faster than even our fastest rocket ships can go. But the farther a planet is from the Sun, the weaker the Sun's gravitational pull on it and the slower the planet goes. Neptune is so distant from the Sun that it moves along its orbit at a speed of only about 3.3 miles (5.3 km) per second. Mercury, the planet nearest the Sun, speeds along at nearly 30 miles (48 km) per second.

A Distant World

There are four giant planets: Jupiter, Saturn, Uranus, and Neptune. Neptune is the most distant and the smallest of them, but it is still about 30,000 miles (49,000 km) across — almost four times wider than Earth. It is about 2.8 billion miles (4.5 billion km) from the Sun, 30 times farther from the Sun than we are.

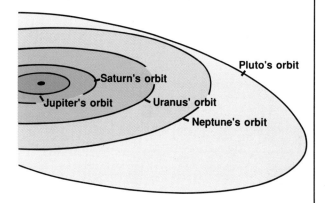

The orbits of the five outermost planets of our Solar system. Within Jupiter's orbit lie the asteroid belt and the orbits of Mars, Earth, Venus, and Mercury.

From Neptune, the Sun looks like a very bright star. Neptune gets only 1/900 of the light and warmth that we get from the Sun. Even so, sunshine on Neptune is 450 times brighter than light reflected to Earth from our full Moon.

Neptune has such a large orbit that it takes about 165 Earth years to go around the Sun just once. A "day" on Neptune is only about 18 hours long.

Opposite: a false-color picture of Neptune. Different colors represent different heights in Neptune's atmosphere. The deepest clouds are shaded dark blue; pinkish clouds are the highest.

Unlike Earth (right), which is one of the Solar system's "rocky" planets, Neptune is a "gas giant," a ball of gases that just gets thicker the deeper down you look. Neptune has no solid surface.

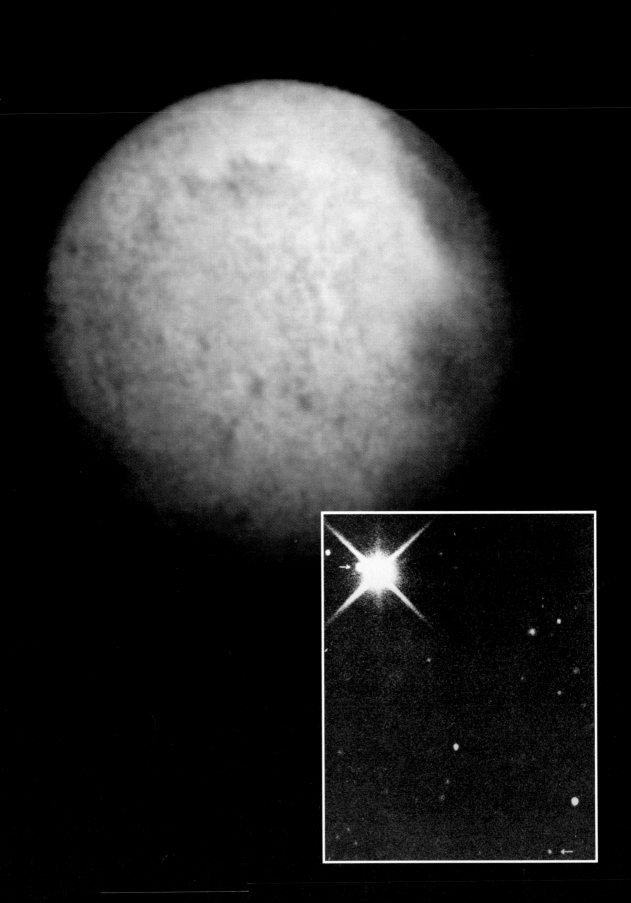

Neptune's "Old" Satellites

Soon after Neptune was discovered, astronomers found a satellite circling it. The moon was named Triton, after the son of Poseidon, the sea god of ancient Greek myths.

Triton is a large satellite, about 78 percent the diameter of our Moon, and is about the same distance from Neptune that our Moon is from us. Triton circles Neptune in just under six days. The Earth's Moon circles Earth in about 27 1/3 days. Even though Neptune is much larger than Earth, Triton's orbit takes less time because Neptune has a stronger gravitational pull.

In 1949, a second moon was discovered, Nereid. It is only about 210 miles (340 km) across and is much farther — over 15 times as far — from Neptune than Triton is. It takes Nereid 360 days — almost one Earth year — to go around Neptune. This is about as long as it takes our Earth to orbit the Sun.

Opposite: This distant glimpse of Triton's speckled surface hints that the moon may have some unusual features. Voyager 2 used special filters to produce this false-color photo. Inset: a photo of Neptune showing Triton (top arrow) and Nereid (bottom right), the only moons of Neptune detected before 1989.

Triton and Nereid, two of Neptune's moons, orbit the planet in strangely cockeyed paths. Nereid travels around Neptune in a wide, oval-shaped orbit. Triton is unlike most of the Solar system's other moons in two ways: it orbits Neptune in a clockwise direction, and its orbit is tilted at an angle to the planet's equator. The straight line shows the direction of Neptune's path around the Sun.

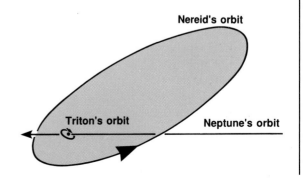

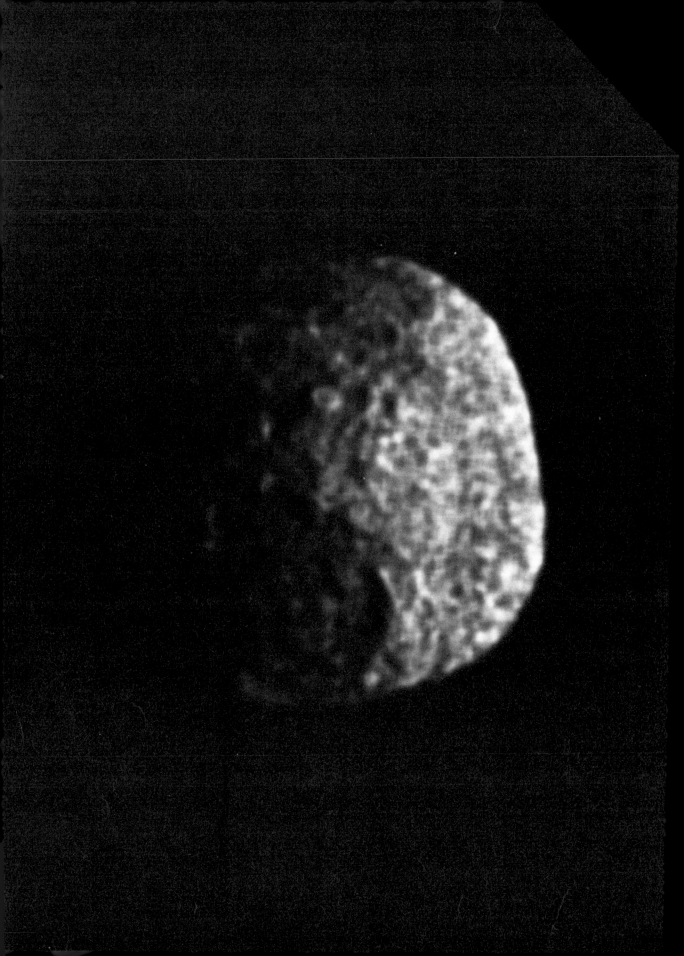

Voyager Update: The "New" Satellites

Neptune is so far from us that it is hard to see small objects very close to it. But Voyager 2 passed near Neptune in August 1989, and it spotted six more satellites circling Neptune. They are all quite close to Neptune and are estimated to be anywhere from 30 to 260 miles (50 to 420 km) across. They are all quite dark and reflect only small amounts of light. That — plus their small size and great distance from Earth — is why they couldn't be seen from Earth.

Like all the other known smaller satellites in the Solar system, Neptune's newly discovered moons are lumpy and irregular. Only large bodies have enough gravitation to force themselves into a round shape.

Opposite: Neptune's second largest known satellite, temporarily named 1989 N1, is a gray, cratered ball. Before Voyager 2 detected 1989 N1, Nereid had been thought to be Neptune's second largest moon.

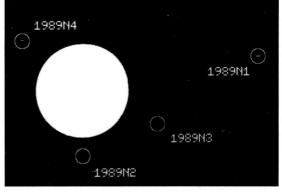

Four of Neptune's six "new" moons appear in the Voyager 2 image at right, and the remaining two are shown in the picture below.

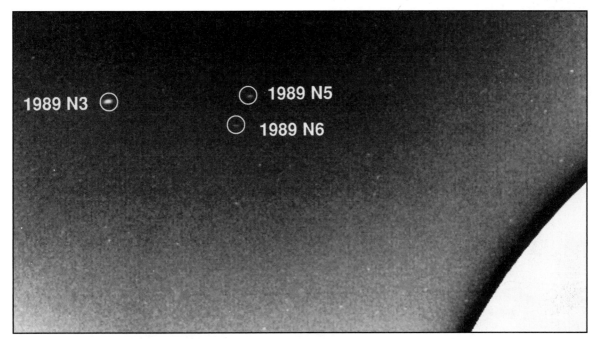

Of rings we sing

There are four giant planets in the
Solar system, and every one of them
has rings. The rings of Jupiter,
Uranus, and Neptune are all thin and
faint and made up of dark particles
that can't really be seen from Earth.
It took space probes to prove they
exist. Yet Saturn has many broad
rings made of bright particles, and
these can be seen from Earth
through even a small telescope.
The mystery is not why planets
have rings, but why Saturn alone
has such large, magnificent rings.

?

Voyager Update:
The Rings of Neptune

Astronomers have found that when Neptune moves in front of a star, that star's light dims a little just before Neptune covers it. Scientists felt this meant there might be rings around Neptune. These didn't seem to be complete rings, however, because stars dimmed as they got close to one side of Neptune, but not to the other.

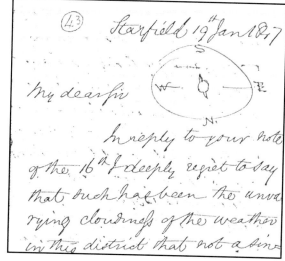

A sketch of Neptune's supposed "ring," as shown in a British letter written in early 1847. Shortly after Neptune's discovery, some astronomers reported a ring around the planet. In reality, the rings are much too faint to be seen from Earth.

As Voyager 2 passed Neptune, it showed that there were three complete rings around the planet. They were thin, without much material in them. They were also clumpy, and the clumps hid the stars more than other parts of the rings did. That's why the rings looked like arcs, rather than full rings, from Earth.

Opposite: The clumps of material in Neptune's rings are obvious in this Voyager 2 picture. Below: Long exposures by Voyager's cameras make Neptune look like a bright glare at the center of this picture, but they clearly show off the Neptune ring system.

Silvery bands of methane clouds cast shadows on a deeper cloud deck.

Voyager Update: The Winds of Neptune

Just as the Sun drives Earth's weather, so the winds of the other planets would seem to be powered by the heat of the Sun. Saturn is farther from the Sun than Jupiter, so Saturn gets less heat and has less violent winds than Jupiter. Uranus, farther still, is quite a quiet planet, as Voyager 2 showed in 1986. It was expected that Neptune would be quieter still.

But Voyager 2 found that the winds of Neptune were surprisingly violent. They moved at speeds of over 400 miles (640 km) an hour. Neptune seems almost as active as Jupiter, even though Neptune gets only 1/20 as much energy from the Sun as Jupiter does.

Background: In this artist's concept, we see how Neptune's atmosphere might distort and multiply the image of the setting Sun. Our view is from just above Neptune's Great Dark Spot.

Neptune — one far-out planet

Neptune takes almost 165 years to orbit the Sun, so it has not yet completed a single circuit since its discovery in 1846. And it won't come back to the place where it was first seen until 2011. Pluto, which takes 250 years to orbit the Sun, is usually the farthest known planet. But during one 20-year period in Pluto's orbit it is a bit closer to the Sun than Neptune is. We are in that period now, so until 1999, Neptune is the farthest planet from the Sun.

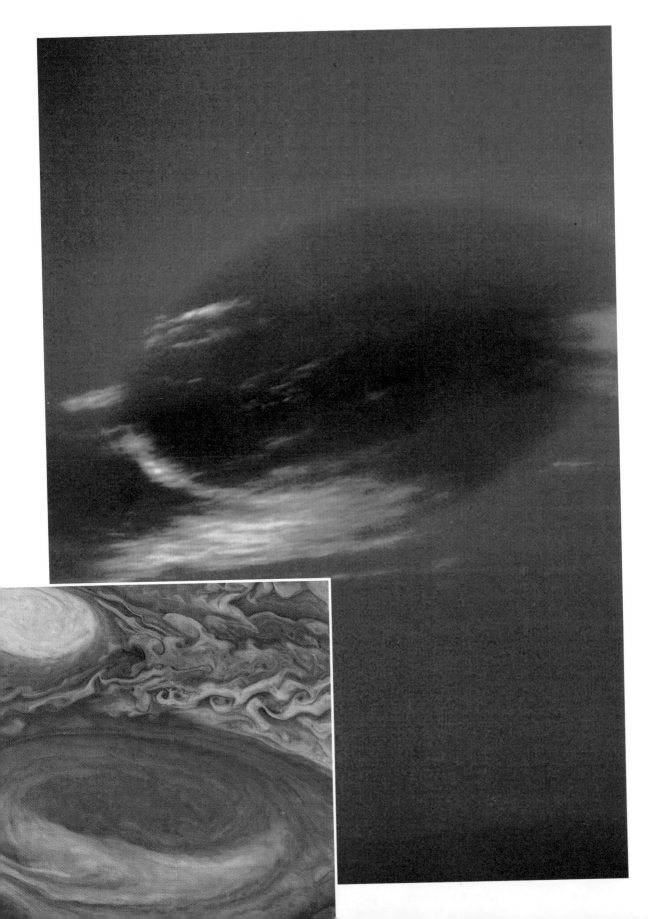

Voyager Update:
The Great Dark Spot

Voyager 2 showed that Neptune is full of surprises. But perhaps Voyager's most astonishing discovery was that Neptune has something in its atmosphere that is much like the Great Red Spot on Jupiter.

Neptune's Great Dark Spot is located in just about the same part of the planet as Jupiter's spot and has the same shape as Jupiter's spot. But Neptune's spot seems to be a deep blue in

Giant Jupiter is no longer the only planet known to have a giant storm. The Great Red Spot, seen here in Jupiter's southern hemisphere, is strikingly similar to Neptune's dark oval.

color with a slight reddish tint. It is smaller than Jupiter's spot, because Neptune is smaller than Jupiter. But if Neptune were scaled to match Jupiter in size, the spots would be the same size, too.

Like Jupiter's red spot, Neptune's dark spot seems to be a never-ending giant hurricane. Its width is about the same as Earth's diameter. In Voyager 2 pictures, scientists saw that bright, thin cirruslike clouds move over the Great Dark Spot. This proves that the spot is lower in Neptune's atmosphere than the clouds!

Opposite: Neptune's Great Dark Spot, as seen by Voyager 2 from a distance of 1.7 million miles (2.8 million km). Methane gas streaming over the spot forms the ever-present white clouds. Inset: Jupiter's Great Red Spot, seen here in a Voyager 1 image, is about three times as wide as Earth.

17

Voyager Update: Neptune's Magnetic Field

Jupiter has a magnetic field that is much stronger than Earth's. Saturn and Uranus have magnetic fields, too. And how about Neptune? Yes! Voyager 2 detected a magnetic field about Neptune as well.

In order to have a magnetic field, a gaseous giant must have a liquid region in its interior that conducts electricity. On the whole, Neptune seems like the other giant planets. It is made up mostly of gaseous substances that get hot and dense in the interior. It might have a small rocky core surrounded by an "ocean" of super-dense, super-hot matter. But some scientists think that the source of Neptune's magnetic field may be closer to its surface than to its core.

> ## The case of the tipped magnetic fields
>
> *Scientists think an astronomical body's magnetic field ought to line up with the body's axis of rotation. For some reason, Earth's magnetic field tips a little bit to its axis. Uranus' magnetic field tips way over. Uranus' axis is turned so it seems to be rolling on its side. This might be why its magnetic field is so tilted. But Neptune's axis is much more nearly upright, and yet its magnetic field is badly tipped, too. Why? Scientists aren't sure.* **?**

Right: Voyager scientists were surprised to learn how far the axis of Neptune's magnetic field tilts away from the axis of the planet's rotation — nearly 47°. The diagram also shows that the magnetic field is lopsidedly centered far off the center of Neptune itself.

Opposite: a look inside Neptune. The incredibly hot, super-dense core of rock, ice, and gas is surrounded by a gaseous "envelope." The enlarged section shows the cloud layers of Neptune's stormy atmosphere.

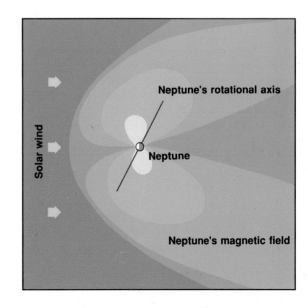

Solar wind

Neptune's rotational axis

Neptune

Neptune's magnetic field

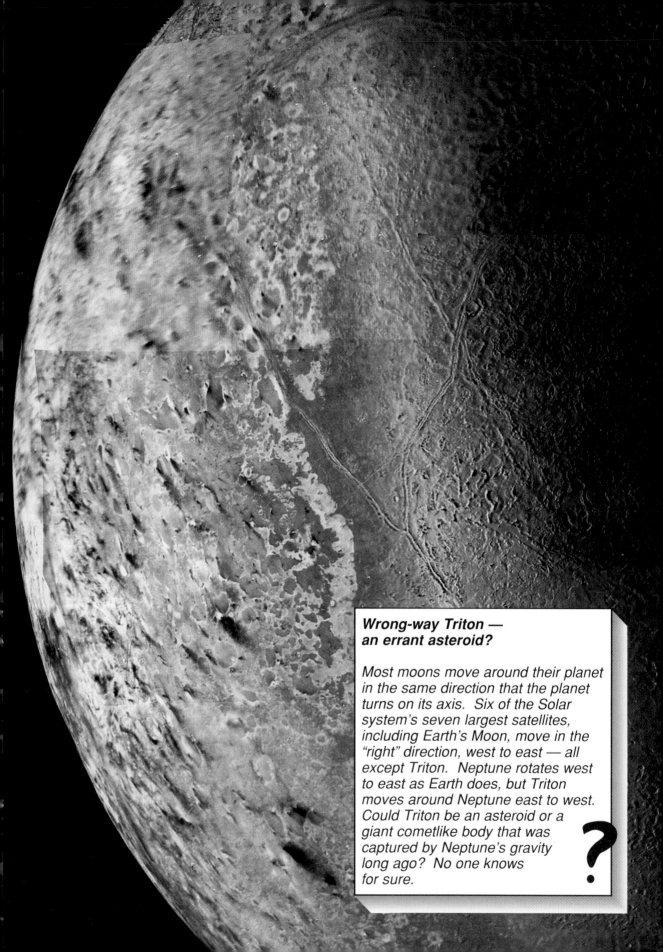

Wrong-way Triton —
an errant asteroid?

*Most moons move around their planet
in the same direction that the planet
turns on its axis. Six of the Solar
system's seven largest satellites,
including Earth's Moon, move in the
"right" direction, west to east — all
except Triton. Neptune rotates west
to east as Earth does, but Triton
moves around Neptune east to west.
Could Triton be an asteroid or a
giant cometlike body that was
captured by Neptune's gravity
long ago? No one knows
for sure.*

?

Voyager Update: A Closer Look at Triton

Voyager 2 also passed near Triton, Neptune's large satellite. Triton's diameter is about 1,700 miles (2,740 km), as compared with our Moon's 2,160 miles (3,480 km). This makes Triton the smallest of the Solar system's seven largest known satellites.

Some scientists expected Triton to be a lot like Saturn's large satellite, Titan. Titan is large enough to hold a hazy atmosphere that hides its surface. But the smaller Triton has only a very thin atmosphere, and so its surface is clearly visible.

Opposite: Scientists combined a dozen Voyager 2 photos to make this image of Triton. Methane ice altered by sunlight may create the pink color.

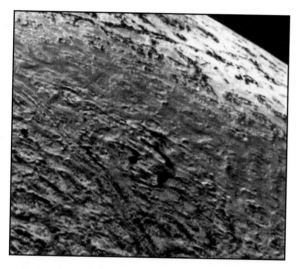

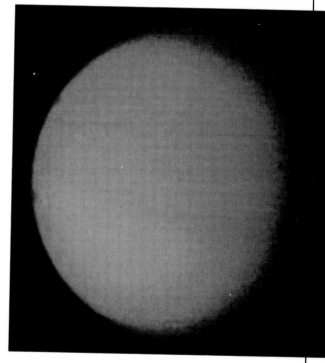

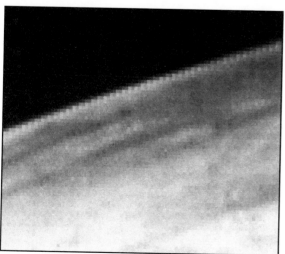

The surface of Titan (above), Saturn's largest moon, hides beneath a hazy atmosphere of methane and nitrogen. Triton's thin atmosphere (bottom left) suspends icy particles that form a thin haze around the satellite. Circular depressions (top left) may be caused by local melting and collapse of Triton's icy surface.

Triton's Surface Revealed

The surface of Triton has a frigid frost of frozen methane and nitrogen on it that reflects the Sun's light. The reflected sunlight gives Triton's icy glaze a pinkish color and makes the satellite brighter than scientists had expected.

Triton is the coldest world we have yet observed, with a temperature of about -400°F (-240°C). This is so cold that nitrogen gas in the atmosphere freezes into an icy frost. Liquid nitrogen underground may erupt into "ice volcanoes" throwing clouds of icy nitrogen and methane into the thin atmosphere. All this adds up to a world whose surface has far more variety to it than the surface of our Moon. Triton may be giving us a hint of what Pluto might look like.

Right: Dark streaks pepper the surface of Triton's south polar cap. They may be from material shot into the atmosphere by "ice volcanoes," jets of liquid nitrogen that shoot up to five miles (8 km) high. Voyager 2 caught several geysers erupting. The sources of the eruptions show up as circular white spots in this photo. Inset: Fault lines cut across portions of Triton's surface.

Opposite: An artist imagines "ice volcanoes" erupting into Triton's thin atmosphere.

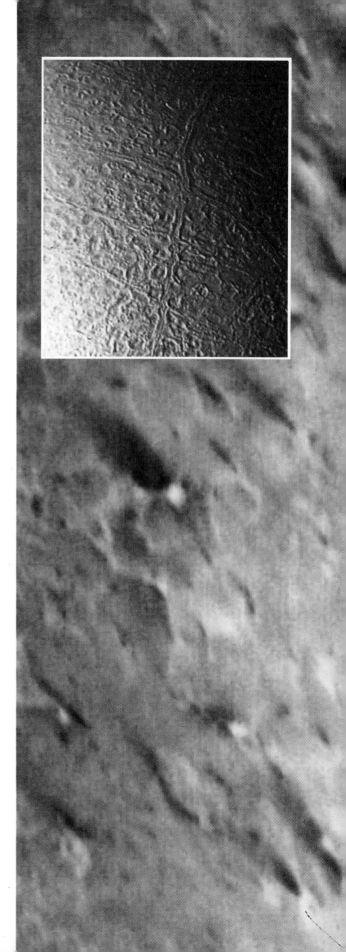

William Herschel

Caroline Herschel

Johann Gottfried Galle

Clyde Tombaugh

Eleanor F. Helin

Beyond Neptune — More to Come?

What lies beyond Neptune in our Solar system? We know about the small world of Pluto and its even smaller satellite, Charon. There are also vast numbers of tiny, icy comets hovering beyond the edges of the known Solar system. But are there any other large planets waiting to be discovered?

Neptune and Pluto do not quite account for all of Uranus' motion, and astronomers have looked for a still farther "Planet X." So far they have found no signs of it. But as Voyager 2 continues to move beyond Neptune and to send back information about the space around it, it is just barely possible that it might detect signs of another super-distant planet.

The discovery of such a planet would be an exciting event here on Earth. But scientists are not especially hopeful about making such a discovery.

Here is a gallery (opposite) of astronomers who have made noteworthy discoveries of objects in our Solar system: British astronomer William Herschel (upper left), who first detected Uranus and several moons of Uranus and Saturn; British astronomer Caroline Herschel (upper right), sister of William and the discoverer of several comets and nebulae; German astronomer Johann Gottfried Galle (center left), who first saw Neptune; US astronomer Clyde Tombaugh (center right), who discovered Pluto in 1930 after studying hundreds of photographs; and astronomer Eleanor F. Helin of the United States (lower left), who has spotted numerous asteroids, including the first asteroid found to have an orbit entirely within that of Earth. There may not be any planets left to discover in our Solar system. But who knows how many asteroids and comets, some of which can come quite close to Earth, remain to be discovered?

> **Sometimes two wrongs _do_ make a right!**
>
> _When Adams and Leverrier calculated Neptune's position, they didn't really know how big it might be, or how far beyond Uranus it might be. Each incorrectly guessed that Neptune was much farther away than it really is, and much larger than it really is. But these two mistakes canceled each other, so each ended up predicting that Neptune would be where it really was. If they had made only one of those mistakes, they would have had a completely wrong answer!_ ●

Voyager 2 — Our Beacon in the Cosmos

Even if Voyager 2 does not spot a distant planet, it will beam back a wealth of information about surrounding space. It will tell us how far out the Sun's stream of charged particles called the solar wind penetrates. Voyager should also report back to us at the point where it enters interstellar space, the "empty" space between the stars.

Scientists have traced the path Voyager 2 will follow for the next million years. By then, it will be 50 light-years away, about 12 times farther away than the nearest star other than our Sun. But in all the time it takes to travel that far, Voyager will never meet up with another star. Its nearest approach to any star other than our Sun will be no closer than 1.65 light-years, almost 10 trillion miles (16 trillion km).

Of course, we don't know what unexpected surprises await Voyager as it sails through the cosmos. But for now, Neptune holds the prize for supplying exciting news beamed back home by our faithful robot.

Opposite: an artist's concept of a future Neptune probe. It will be some time before spacecraft again visit Neptune. And yet, we have done rather well. In the 30 years since the first satellite orbited Earth, craft from our planet have visited every known planet in the Solar system except Pluto.

Fact File: Neptune

Neptune is our Solar system's fourth largest known planet. It is also the eighth closest to the Sun. Only tiny Pluto has an orbit that stretches farther from the Sun than Neptune's. In fact, Neptune is so far from the Sun that its "year" equals nearly 165 Earth years. And for about 20 of those years, Pluto's extremely eccentric, or non-circular, orbit takes it within Neptune's orbit. This means that Neptune is then farther from the Sun than Pluto is!

With the journey of Voyager 2 past Neptune in 1989, many mysteries of this cold and beautiful planet were cleared up, and many previously unknown secrets were revealed. One mystery, that of Neptune's "arcs," was cleared up when Voyager showed the arcs to be rings — thin, clumpy rings that were only partly visible to telescopes on Earth.

Future missions to the outer reaches of the Solar system are probably many years off. So it is not likely that any planet will soon show off nearly as much — and in such spectacular fashion — as Neptune did in 1989.

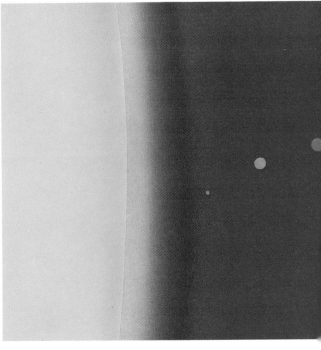

Above: the Sun and its Solar system family, left to right: Mercury, Venus, Earth, Mars, Jupiter, Saturn, Uranus, Neptune, and Pluto.

The Moons of Neptune

Name	Diameter	Distance from Neptune
Triton	1,690 miles (2,720 km)	220,300 miles (354,460 km)
Nereid	211 miles (340 km)	3,424,300 miles (5,509,700 km)

Neptune: How It Measures Up to Earth

Planet	Diameter	Rotation Period
Neptune	30,200 miles (48,592 km)	17 hours, 42 minutes
Earth	7,926 miles (12,753 km)	23 hours, 56 minutes

The Sun and Its Family of Planets

Right: Here is a close-up of Neptune and its known moons. Thanks to Voyager, we now know that Neptune has several more moons than had been previously detected from Earth.

ame	Diameter	Distance from Neptune	Name	Diameter	Distance from Neptune
989 N1	260 miles (420 km)	73,000 miles (117,600 km)	1989 N4	100 miles (160 km)	38,500 miles (62,000 km)
989 N2	120 miles (190 km)	45,700 miles (73,600 km)	1989 N5	55 miles (90 km)	31,000 miles (50,000 km)
989 N3	90 miles (145 km)	32,600 miles (52,500 km)	1989 N6	30 miles (48 km)	30,000 miles (48,200 km)

riod of Orbit round Sun ngth of year)	Known Moons	Surface Gravity	Distance from Sun (nearest-farthest)	Least Time It Takes for Light to Travel to Earth
164 years, 288 days	8	1.13*	2.7-2.8 billion miles (4.3-4.5 billion km)	3 hours, 53 minutes
23 hours, 56 minutes	1	1.00*	92-95 million miles (148-153 million km)	—

*Multiply your weight by this number to find out how much you would weigh on this planet.

More Books About Neptune

Here are more books that contain information about Neptune. If you are interested in them, check your library or bookstore.

Astronomy Today: Planets, Stars, Space Exploration. Moche (Random House)
Our Solar System. Asimov (Gareth Stevens)
The Planets. Barrett (Franklin Watts)
The Planets. Couper (Franklin Watts)
The Planets: Exploring the Solar System. Gallant (Four Winds/Macmillan)

Places to Visit

You can explore Neptune and other places in the Universe without leaving Earth. Here are some museums and centers where you can find many different kinds of space exhibits.

Benedum Natural Science Center
Wheeling, West Virginia

Casper Planetarium
Casper, Wyoming

University of Saskatchewan Observatory
Saskatoon, Saskatchewan

Oregon Museum of Science and Technology/
  Kendall Planetarium
Portland, Oregon

Wetherbee Planetarium
Albany, Georgia

Grengas Planetarium
Science Museum of Connecticut
West Hartford, Connecticut

Climenhaga Observatory
University of Victoria
Victoria, British Columbia

Ronald E. McNair Space Theater
Russell Davis Planetarium
Jackson, Mississippi

For More Information About Neptune

Here are some people you can write to for more information about Neptune. Be sure to tell them exactly what you want to know about. And include your full name and address so they can write back to you.

For information about Neptune:
National Space Society
600 Maryland Avenue SW
Washington, DC 20024

Space Communications Branch
Ministry of State for Science and Technology
240 Sparks Street, C. D. Howe Building
Ottawa, Ontario K1A 1A1, Canada

For catalogs of posters, slides, and other astronomy materials:
AstroMedia Order Department
21027 Crossroads Circle
Waukesha, Wisconsin 53187

Sky Publishing Corporation
49 Bay State Road
Cambridge, Massachusetts 02238-1290

Selectory Sales
Astronomical Society of the Pacific
1290 24th Avenue
San Francisco, California 94122

About Voyager 2's mission to Neptune:
NASA Jet Propulsion Laboratory
Public Affairs 180-201, 4800 Oak Grove Drive
Pasadena, California 91109

Glossary

atmosphere: the gases that surround a planet, star, or moon. Neptune's atmosphere is ice cold and incredibly windy, with wind speeds of up to 400 mph (640 kph).

axis: the imaginary straight line about which a planet, star, or moon turns or spins.

billion: in North America — and in this book — the number represented by 1 followed by nine zeroes: 1,000,000,000. In some places, such as the United Kingdom (Britain), this number is called "a thousand million." In these places, one billion would then be represented by 1 followed by *12* zeroes: 1,000,000,000,000 — a million million, a number known as a trillion in North America.

diameter: the length of a straight line through the exact center of a circle or sphere. Neptune has a diameter of about 30,000 miles (49,000 km).

giant planets: Jupiter, Saturn, Uranus, and Neptune — the four largest known planets in our Solar system. Also called the gas giants, these planets are made up mostly of gases and lie beyond the asteroid belt that encircles the four inner rocky planets, Mercury, Venus, Mars, and Earth.

gravity: the force that causes astronomical bodies to be attracted to one another and that holds them in their orbits.

Great Dark Spot: a large storm in Neptune's atmosphere, similar to Jupiter's Great Red Spot.

light-year: the distance that light travels in one year — nearly six trillion miles (9.6 trillion km).

magnetic field: the force that surrounds a planet like an "atmosphere" of energy. Earth's magnetic field allows compasses to work.

methane: a colorless, odorless, flammable gas.

Neptune: the ancient Roman god of the sea (called Poseidon by the ancient Greeks). The planet Neptune is named for him because of its watery blue-green color.

"Planet X": a possible tenth planet some scientists believe may exist somewhere out beyond the orbit of Pluto.

rings: thin bands of rock, ice, and dust that circle all the gas giants. Of the four giant planets, Saturn has the most clearly visible rings. They can be seen from Earth through binoculars or a small telescope.

rotation: the act of turning about a central point on an axis.

satellite: a smaller body orbiting a larger body. The Moon is Earth's natural satellite. Sputnik 1 was Earth's first artificial satellite.

Solar wind: tiny particles that travel from the Sun's surface at a speed of 300 miles (480 km) a second.

Voyager 2: the space probe that journeyed past Neptune in 1989, beaming back to Earth pictures and information about Neptune.

Index

The publishers wish to thank the following for permission to reproduce copyright material: front cover, © Bob Eggleton,
1990; pp. 4, 6, 8 (inset), 10, 11 (both), 12, 13 (lower), 14 (inset), 16 (full page), 20, 21 (all), 23 (both), Jet Propulsion
Laboratory; pp. 5 (both), 8 (full page), 24 (middle left and upper right), courtesy of Yerkes Observatory; pp. 7 (upper), 9, 19,
Sharon Burris, © Gareth Stevens, Inc., 1990; pp. 7 (lower), 16 (inset), 17, courtesy of NASA; p. 13 (top), collection of Richard
Baum; pp. 14-15 (lower spread), © Sally J. Bensusen, 1989; pp. 18, 22, © Paul Dimare, 1989; p. 24 (upper left), National
Maritime Museum; p. 24 (lower left), courtesy of Eleanor F. Helin; p. 24 (middle right), New Mexico State University; p. 26,
© Pat Rawlings, 1989; pp. 28-29 (upper spread), © Sally J. Bensusen; p. 29 (inset), © Thomas O. Miller/Studio "X," 1990.